Content

Epoxy Casting Resin – The Ultimate Guide for Resin Casting

Casting resins are specially developed epoxy resins, which are designed for casting molds, figures, jewellery and some other applications. We show you where a casting resin should be used and what to consider when buying a casting resin.

Content

What is Casting Resin?

Casting resin is a low-viscosity epoxy resin, which consists of two components: the actual resin and the matching hardener. When these two components are mixed, a chemical reaction occurs, which causes the mass to harden for some time. And this brings us to the special features of casting resin – its thin consistency. This property allows the resin to penetrate and fill even the smallest gaps and cavities. The thinner consistency also has an influence on the curing time, which is considerably longer. With the casting resin, we therefore have a highly specialised product for very specific applications.

Buy Casting Resin – The best Resin in Comparison

There is a large number of different resins available for purchase. Unfortunately, manufacturers often use different terms, making it difficult to distinguish between casting resins and epoxy resins. Terms such as laminating resin or gel / topcoat are also frequently used, which can lead to costly mispurchases. We have compared the best casting resins with each other and compared them in a clearly arranged table.

The Differences Between Casting Resin and Epoxy Resin

Casting Resin

Low viscosity consistency Significantly longer curing times Therefore longer processing times.
With casting resin thicker layers can be cast
Due to the thin consistency, layers of paint mix quickly

Epoxy Resin

More viscous consistency Faster
curing times
Relatively short processing times
Only thin layers up to a maximum of 2cm possible
ink layers remain rather separated and can be controlled better

Coloring Casting Resin

Casting resin can be colored like epoxy resin with color pastes, alcohol inks and color pigments. Our guidebook **coloring epoxy resin** presents these in detail and gives many tips for application.

Since casting resin is low viscous, i.e. thin-bodied, different layers of paint mix faster than with epoxy resin. applications, but for example in resin art a good color separation is important.

Casting Resin Molds

The fastest way to start with Resin casting is using silicone molds. They are available in di fferent shapes and sizes – from small resin casting molds for producing resin jewelry to big molds for casting spheres and other geometric shapes.

Maximum possible Layer Thickness

Casting resins usually cure much more slowly, so they produce less heat. This allows significantly thicker casting layers of up to 10 centimeters. The maximum amount that can be processed at once is also increased, so that depending on the product, up to 10 kg can be processed at once. However, please note the manufacturer's instructions, as there are also products with which a maximum of 5 centimetres thick layer can be cast at once.

The heat development is generally a very important issue, because if the layer is too thick or too large, epoxy resin in particular can become so hot that it can cause burns. The quality of the cured mixture also suffers, so that total damage to the project can be the result. If the casting resin also becomes too hot due to the exothermic reaction, toxic fumes are released.Therefore, always wear protective clothing and a breathing mask.

Curing Times

Casting resins need up to one week to cure completely. The huge advantage lies in the processing time: If epoxy resin can only be processed for a few minutes up to one hour, Resin Casting Resin offers products with a processing time of up to 24 hours. This has several positive effects:
For larger areas, this leaves more time for casting and embedding
Especially with large quantities of resin with different colors a lot of time is needed
Air bubbles can escape much longer due to the open time

> Apart from the greater patience until the project is finished, there are basically no disadvantages as long as the casting resin is also used for the correct application.

Instructions for Resin Casting Application

Preparation of your Resin Casting

Provide all necessary materials so that they are always at hand
Protect the workplace with a cardboard or plastic sheet
If you want to pour out wood or other materials,tape off any holes well so that the resin remains where you want it to be. It is always astonishing where the thin-bodied casting resin finds a way where it does not belong. If you want to cast objects or pour wood, seal the surface with a little epoxy resin first.
Read the cast resin manufacturer's instructions regarding mixing ratio and other safety-relevant information
Protect yourself with the appropriate protective clothing, safety goggles, nit rile gloves and breathing mask

Mixing Epoxy Casting Resin

Weigh resin and hardener accurately
Mix both components carefully and for a few minutes

If you want to color the epoxy casting resin, add the color paste or color pigments and mix the whole thing again thoroughly
Let the whole thing stand for one minuteso that some of the air mixed in can escape
Pour the resin mixture into the moldor the cavity to be filled
AnyairbubblescanberemovedwithahotairdryeroraButaneTorch

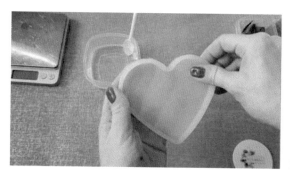 

Casting Objects

If you want to cast objects, first pour a small amount of resin
Then place the objects to be poured in with a toothpick or wooden spatula
With heavy materials, the first layer should already be dry so that they do not sink to the bottom
Fill up the mold generously afterwards, as the material may shrink a little during curing

Clear Casting Resin - How to Achieve transparent Results .

If you do not want to color your casting resin, then for most applications it is desired that the casting resin hardens crystal clear.

Tip: Even if all these points are observed, it is important to know that no casting resin is completely immune to yellowing over time. Especially when used outdoors in wind and weather, this cannot be prevented to a certain extent.

ANTHONY PAZ / shutterstock.com

Use high quality clear casting resin products from brand manufacturers Pay attention to a high-quality UV filter. Exact compliance with the mixing ratio Coating with an additional varnish with UV filter can give better results

Hardness of the Surface

In general it can be said that epoxy resin surfaces are harder than those of cast resins. This need not always be a bad thing, because lower hardness means more flexibility, which can be a great advantage especially when working with wood, glass or other changing materials. For example, wood shrinks due to changing temperatures or humidity. It is important to consider whether these properties are desired or not. For a table or a surface with a high mechanical load, an epoxy resin, which forms a hard and abrasion-resistant layer, is the better choice. It is therefore worth applying a layer of epoxy resin as a finish to achieve better mechanical strength, for example on a wooden table.

For which Applications is Casting Resin suitable?

In order not to suffer any setbacks, you should always consider using the right product before pouring resin. Cast resin can be used for the following applications:

Cast resin table /River Table Resin
Jewellery
Pouring into silicone molds or other molds To fill
wood with epoxy resin

Weigh and Mix Epoxy Resin

To mix resin and hardener in the perfect ratio, it is worth using a digital scale. For cast resin systems which are mixed by volume, a suitable measuring cup will help.

What is Resin Casting?

Working with epoxy resin has been an integral part of the DIY scene for some time now. Absolutely hip in this area is the so-called "Resin Casting", in which various objects such as natural materials, small stones or glitter etc. are embedded in epoxy resin.

To give the resin an attractive shape, the desired elements are poured into a plastic mold together with a suitable resin. molds made of silicone have proven to be particularly suitable, as they are extremely flexible and thus make it much easier to loosen the work piece after curing. The absolute top class here are polished silicone molds. Their smooth, shiny surface on the inside guarantees an even, glossy result, where further finishing such as sleeping or polishing is usually unnecessary.

© Jane Lenahan / Maia and the Wildflower

Frequently Asked Questions and Answers

How long does Casting Resin need to harden?

This varies greatly depending on the product and formulation. Casting resin also has a longer drying time of approx. 24 to 48 hours due to the longer open time compared to epoxy resin.

What can be poured into Casting Resin?

You can cast all materials in casting resin. Materials that contain air, such as wood or other porous materials, should be sealed with a thin layer of epoxy resin in advance to prevent air bubbles from escaping during pouring, which can be difficult to remove.

How stable is Casting Resin?

Casting resin is extremely stable and resilient.Therefore, epoxy resin table tops can also be cast with it without any problems.

How hot does Casting Resin get?

In contrast to laminating resin, casting resin becomes much less hot, as the exothermic reaction is delayed. This is also the great advantage of this material – especially for thicker layers and larger quantities.

Which molds for Casting Resin?

Silicone molds are ideally suited for smaller objects. However, larger areas can also be filled with casting resin, which are surrounded by a wooden construction.

How to Color Resin – The Best Coloring Products for Epoxy

Epoxy resin is very suitable for coloring it and is therefore often used by artists, craftsmen and do-it-yourselfers. Epoxy resin is usually transparent to crystal clear and this is also desired for some applications, for example to cast in objects. For many other applications, however, it is useful or desired to color the liquid.

Which Colors and Pigments are Suitable for Resin?

There are many color media on the market. However, not all of them are suitable for coloring resin. Especially if water is contained in the inks, the mixing ratio changes and the mass may not harden or dull spots may appear. Light resistance is another important criterion. The following inks have proven themselves and can basically be used in all epoxy products:

Color Pigments for Epoxy Resin

Color pigments are a safe way to color resin. If you use high quality pigments, you only need a small amount. Color pigments in powder form do not dissolve completely, resulting in an exciting, slightly granular optical effect. We have summarized the best products in comparison:

Liquid Color Concentrate

Liquid color concentrate can be mixed very easily with epoxy and dissolves completely, giving a very even color. We have also summarized the most proven products in the comparison

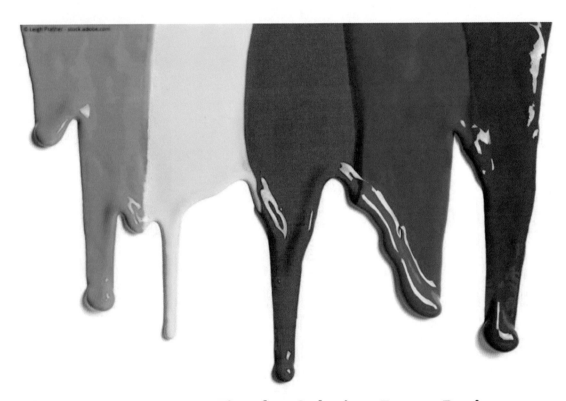

The most Important Tips for Coloring Epoxy Resin

The mixing ratio is a very important factor with resin. If something changes in the composition between resin and hardener, unforeseen problems can occur. The addition of color changes the composition, so there are a few points to consider.

□

Only use highly pigmented or concentrated paints in order not to negatively influence the mixing ratio
Only use paints that do not contain water
First test with a small amount of resin and paint to see if both the color and the reaction of the resin meet your expectations

Coloring resin does not replace UV protection. The yellowing of epoxy resins without UV protection is of course less noticeable than that of uncolored, transparent resin, but the lack of protection can cause the color to fade and the yellowing changes the shade First process your resin uncolored to get a feeling for the handling and to get to know the specific properties. You will then be able to assess to what extent the additional color changes the properties

Coloring Epoxy Resin – Tutorial

Get the best results with this step-by-step guide:
Provide all materials, since the time factor always plays a role when working with resin Cover your workplace cleanly so that no traces are left behind
Wearing nitrile gloves, protective goggles and a breathing mask is strongly recommended
Resin and hardener are carefully mixed in the correct ratio. A sufficient mixing is important.
Then mix the ready paint into the epoxy resin . Start with a small amount of color pigments or liquid color concentrate and mix well. Repeat this step until the desired color intensity is achieved.
Be careful not to add too much color, as this will change the mixing ratio. The rule of thumb is a maximum of five percent.

© honey_inside - stock.adobe.com

Epoxy Resin Color: All Color Media Presented in Detail

Paste-like Consistency / Liquid Colors

Special Colorants for Resins

There are some liquid colorants specially developed for use with resin. They are very suitable for dyeing. Here is one of the best known ResinTint from the manufacturer ArtResin, which offers highest quality and is extremely productive.

Acrylic Paint

The acrylic paint consists of color pigments, binders and water as well as other additives for durability, depending on the manufacturer and product. We do not recommend the use of acrylic paint, as the additives and water contained in it can lead to unforeseen results. In addition, one often gets a dull surface or streaks.

Alcohol Ink

Ink is usually based on water as a solvent, but there are also alcoholic inks. Both variants offer an extremely high pigmentation, so that only a few drops are sufficient to color the epoxy resin. The light fastness of Alcohol Inks is also generally less good, making them unsuitable for outdoor use. Alcohol Inks are transparent and highly concentrated.

Airbrush Paint

Airbrush paint has proven to be very suitable for combination with epoxy resin. Here, however, you should pay attention to high-quality products, as only here the color concentration is sufficiently high. An extremely recommendable product here are the airbrush colors from Aerosol by Schmincke.

Oil Paint

Due to the lipids it contains, oil paint cannot be mixed with casting resin, as the liquids do not combine with each other and the result is lump formation.

Watercolors

Watercolors are generally not suitable in combination with resin. The main reason is the low pigmentation – the color simply does not color enough. So an extremely large amount of watercolor would be necessary to achieve a sufficient coloration. The hard consistency also means that the paint cannot really be mixed in.

Color Pigments and Powdery Additives

Color Pigments

Color pigments are available in different versions: From normal, matte colors to metallic pigments that shimmer. It is important to note here that the pigments have a high light resistance so that they do not fade. There are some established manufacturers of color pigments which offer a high quality. Noname products should definitely be avoided here.

© Csák István - stock.adobe.com

Glowing Pigments

For the additional wow-effect you can also use additional luminous pigments which glow in the dark. There are both pigments that glow under black light and those that are "charged" by UV light and then glow in the dark.

Glitter Powder

You can also create exciting effects with glitter powder in all variations: From classic metallic glitter to holographic glitter, there are no limits to your fantasy. These do not color your casting resin, but give your works an additional eye-catching effect.

Can Epoxy Resin also be Painted with Color?

Yes this is possible. However, the use of a high-quality two-component paint is recommended, for example a car paint. Normally, however, it makes sense to color the resin directly during casting.
There are, however, applications where it makes sense to paint, for example in terrariums or aquariums.

Pouring synthetic resin Step by step guide

Preparation of equipment and materials

The procedure is explained here using the example of a decorative heart with dried flowers, natural materials and mica flakes.

First of all, you should place all the materials and tools you need so that you have them handy. Resin for resin casting is delivered with detailed information and manufacturer's instructions regarding the exact processing method and important safety instructions. Please read this information carefully before you start working.
This is especially true if you have little or no experience in processing epoxy resin. Due to the fact that the material of different manufacturers can also have different properties in further processing, this procedure is extremely important. Safety glasses, gloves and respiratory protection should be mandatory for your own safety when using the resin. You should also cover the working environment with e.g. a foil to protect it from damage caused by the resin.

Mixing the Resin Resin

In our example we use a 2-part low viscosity epoxy resin. This is always mixed in the ratio 2 : 1. Here too, however, manufacturer-related differences are possible, so please observe the manufacturer's instructions. To make the bubbles in the resin disappear, let it stand for about one minute after mixing. Alternatively, you can also briefly (!) wave a hot-air dryer over them.

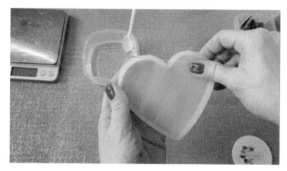 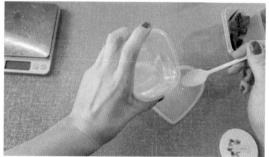

Pouring the base

To avoid later contamination of the finished part, thoroughly clean the mold used from dust, stains or foreign matter before pouring the resin. Only then start resin casting of the first layer. In our example, we want to produce a decorative heart that is only a few centimeters high and is therefore only cast from two layers.

If you would like to cast a larger piece with a deeper mold, you will have to work in several layers. It is essential to pay attention to the manufacturer's instructions on the packaging, as the maximum thickness of a layer can vary depending on the brand of epoxy resin.

Positioning of the decorative elements

After you have poured the first layer of epoxy resin, the so-called base, remove the bubbles that have formed in the same way as when mixing. The decorative elements of your choice are then placed on this base. Besides the dried flowers, natural materials and mica flakes, in our example a small plastic dragonfly is used.

We put the elements into the still liquid resin, as this is a very light material. If you want to use heavier things like crystals or stones, the whole thing has to be put on the already dried resin to prevent the material from sinking. By this procedure you give the impression that the objects are "floating" in the resin.

Under certain circumstances, small air bubbles may form around the objects when they are inserted. However, these can be easily removed by moving the elements back and forth and carefully pushing them down. A toothpick is very useful for this. There are of course no limits to creativity when selecting and positioning the decorative elements.

Tip: Elements with a "chocolate side", as is the case with flowers, for example, should be placed in the resin with this side facing down. The reason for this is that the underside of the silicone mold will later be the "beautiful" front side of the piece.

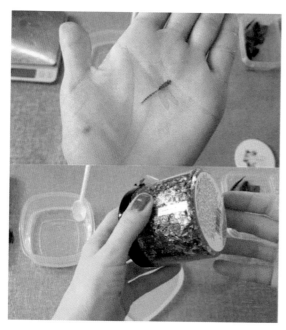

Allow the first layer to cure

Now the base should dry thoroughly. If necessary, new bubbles may form in the epoxy resin, which should be removed before curing. As it often happens that the inserted decorative elements shift just at the beginning of the hardening, please make sure that they stay in place. Regarding the curing time, please observe the manufacturer's instructions. Some manufacturers recommend not applying the second layer until the base is completely dry. Others, on the other hand, recommend pouring the second layer on top of the not yet fully cured layer, as this allows the individual layers to bond better.

Casting the second resin layer

For resin casting of the second layer, you must first mix new casting resin after the base has cured or dried. Proceed in the same way as with the first mixture. After mixing, you should go over the finished resin with a hot-air dryer to remove any bubbles. Then fill the mold completely with the epoxy resin. To prevent the formation of bubbles, the hot-air blow-dryer is also used here again. Another advantage of this procedure: If there are badly mixed parts in the resin, this prevents them from "floating up" and leaving a sticky layer on the surface of the finished piece. Even during this phase you should always make sure that the mold is free of dust and hairs. While the second layer is drying, it is also advisable to check again and again whether bubbles have formed in the resin. These can then be removed immediately.

Release from the mold

After the curing time recommended by the manufacturer, please check if the resin is actually sufficiently dry to release it from the mold. This is the case if it is not yet completely hard, but also no longer sticky. Caution is required when releasing. Since the element is not yet completely hardened at this point, it is quite possible that it will bend slightly during this process. If this is the case, the object must be carefully restored to its original shape before final curing. It is important that the release is carried out on a clean, smooth and even
surface.

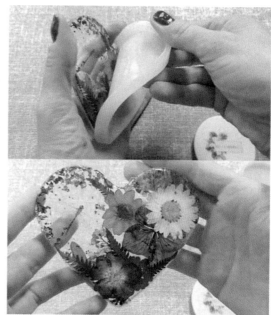

images: © Jane Lenahan / Maia and the Wildflower

Last but not least: The Finish

After release, the edges of the cast unique specimen may be slightly rough and sharp-edged on the back. However, this can easily be corrected with a fine micro mesh or simple sandpaper. If you have worked with a polished silicone mold, the work itself usually does not need to be reground, as these molds are extremely smooth and shiny and produce an almost perfectly smooth surface. We have prepared detailed instructions for you on the subject of grinding and polishing epoxy resin.

When sanding the edges, you should therefore only take care not to slip off accidentally and damage the smooth surface. Now you have the possibility to decorate your finished object, e.g. with a bow or a jute ribbon, by drilling a small hole in the cast piece and passing the decorative ribbon through.

<u>Play video</u>

A little tip at the end: Unique pieces made of epoxy resin and flowers or natural materials should be protected from direct sunlight. Otherwise they could fade and lose some of their luminosity.

Susceptibility to the inclusion of Air Bubbles

Both epoxy resin and cast resin Both materials are equally susceptible to air bubble entrapment. Air bubbles can escape more easily with epoxy resin because it is a thinner layer. This allows the bubbles to rise to the surface faster and thus burst. However, cast resin also has an advantage with regard to air inclusions: Due to the long pot life, the air bubbles have longer time to escape from the cast resin.

But also when working with casting resin, you can make some preparations to avoid air bubbles as far as possible, even with thicker layers. If you are working with porous surfaces such as wood, you can apply a thin layer of epoxy resin in advance. This will seal the surface and prevent air bubbles from escaping from these porous surfaces and getting into the resin.

The same applies to objects that you want to embed in the resin – a sealant always helps to reduce air inclusions in case of doubt.

Resin Rings DIY – Your Guide on how to make Resin Rings

A very popular and easy project to begin with is making resin rings. Follow these easy instructions on how to make your own beautiful resin rings.

Popularity of Resin Rings

If you are a creative person and like venturing into the world of DIY, making your resin rings is a popular and easy option. Most people will quickly learn the techniques needed to make resin rings. There are countless ideas you can realize, also there are endless inspirations you can find on the internet. An advantage is they should last for a very long time, depending on the products you use.

Products and ingredients should be available at most local craft stores, otherwise you can research online for products. The simplest method to make resin rings is to buy or use an available mold. As soon as you have gained a bit of experience in the art of making resin rings, you can start making your molds, which will allow you to customize the ring in unique settings.

There are many videos and tutorials available online that teaches you How to make resin rings, including courses and workshops that will develop and expand this craft.

Supplies needed to make resin rings

Best Resin for Epoxy Rings

You will want a good quality epoxy for your resin jewelry piece so that it will last for as long as possible. You may prefer a casting resin for creating rings, as the thin consistency of this resin makes it the best choice for pouring into molds.

Premium Pick: PROMARINE SUPPLIES Art Resin

This is a premium product, and is therefore a lot more costly than some other resins. This product has been formulated specifically to be used for art-based projects, such as for creating jewelry. Using this resin will result in a clear, glossy finish that will last for a long time.

An easy 1:1 mixing ratio makes this product easy to use for both beginners and experts. You will have approximately 30 to 45 minutes of working time with this resin before it begins to harden, after which it should cure within a standard period of 24 to 72 hours, depending on the piece and its environment.

This epoxy resin is made with top-quality, non-toxic ingredients to make it safe for use both inside and outside. You will not have to worry as much about your resin becoming yellow over time, as this product has a formula that prevents this from happening. Your resin piece will possess a smooth and extremely glossy finish with the utmost shine.

Pros
*Non-toxic
*Self-leveling
*Simple to use
*Resists yellowing *Exceptional shine *Longer working time

Cons
*A little bit pricier

Best Value for Money: ALUMILITE Clear Casting Resin

This casting resin is easy to use, affordable, and will last for a long time. In addition to the resin and its respective hardener, this kit also includes two stirring sticks and three measuring cups. You can use this resin to create any number of detailed ring designs.

With an easy mixing ratio of one part of resin to one part of hardener, you should not have any difficulties creating your epoxy ring. This resin is approved by the FDA to be

used with food after a curing period of seven days.
This resin is better suited to smaller projects as it may yellow over time, particularly if it is frequently exposed to UV light. The resin may give off a relatively strong smell while you are working with it, however.

Pros
*FDA-approved
*Easy to use
*Comes equipped with mixing sticks and measuring cups
*Self-leveling
*Crystal-clear once cured

Cons
*Short shelf-life
*Long curing time
*May yellow over time
*Strong odor

Other materials you will need
•

Proper preparation is very important, so before you begin make sure you have all the materials you will need for this project.
Materials needed to cast Epoxy Resin:

- A Resin Ring Mold (or you can make your own silicone mold)
- Resin dye or Resin compatible pigments
- If you want to make it even more personal, you can also use personal objects to
- embed
- A Resin work mat or wax paper
- Latex gloves
- 3 small measuring cups
  Squeeze condiment bottle (optional)
  Blow Dryer
  Toothpicks and popsicle sticks
  An empty box or container to cover your work
  Quick Drying Adhesive

PRJ / shutterstock.com

How to make resin rings with a bought mold

In this DIY guide to making resin rings with a bought mold, you will learn all the steps to get your first **Resin jewelry** piece.

Preparation

This project kicks off with proper preparation and must be carried out in a well-ventilated workspace. Once you have all your equipment ready on your worktable and laid down your wax paper or resin mat (this is needed for any resin that might drip), you can start making rings. The worktable must be leveled for the resin mixture to remain even during curing.

Put the resin and hardener into warm water as it will help the forming of air bubbles. You can also mix it smoother. Prepare your workspace and make sure you have all tools by hand as you don't have time to waste as you start.

Resin mixing and coloring

Epoxy Resin is an easy medium to work with but read the instructions on the labels carefully. Use your 2 measuring cups to mix equal parts of resin and hardener. Mix it in a mixing container.

The next step is to add resin color to your mixture. Mix and blend completely with a popsicle stick or mixing tool. Add your glitter at this stage. If you are planning to use more than the basic color, mix it in separate cups with your resin mixture.

How to cast your resin ring

Once mixing is completed, the resin must be poured into your mold. For more precise pouring, you can use a condiment bottle.

Add filler: Pour a layer of resin into the mold. Then add the items that you have chosen to the resin. You can add another layer of resin if needed, but be careful not to add too much resin and over-fill your mold. Use a torch or hairdryer on low heat to remove any air bubbles that might be trapped in the resin.

Note: Pour straight into the bevel cup if you use a blank ring as this will only use a small amount of resin.

Let it cure

Allow 24 – 48 hours to fully cure the resin. Cover the mold with a container or box so that no dust or filth can get into your resin during the curing process.

Note: You can use UV Resin, which is ideal for smaller pieces if you don' t want to wait out the curing process. No mixing is needed and it cures within minutes simply by using a UV light.

Demolding

To find out the curing time of your epoxy resin, take a look at the label on your container. You can only remove the items from the mold once the resin has fully cured.

Demold carefully as sharp edges sometimes form. If you have problems with demolding, check if you use a polished mold or use a demolding spray before you put in the resin next time.

Polishing and Finish

Depending on the quality of your mold, it is possible that you will notice some share edges or other imperfections in your unmolded resin ring. The first step to fix these small errors, you can smooth these out with fine-grit sandpaper. More about how to do this, you can find in our resin sanding tutorial.

The next step would be polish your resin piece to create a nice shine to your ring. To add a clear gloss effect, you can use Crystal Clear Resin.

A basic round ring mold forms a solid resin ring and there are many shapes and designs to use and glue onto a ring base.

This piece needs some polishing

withthesehands / shutterstock.com

Making basic resin ring molds

It is not too difficult to make resin ring molds, but it may require a bit of practicing before creating the perfect mold. The easiest method is to buy a Silicone mold-making kit and replicate the rings you want. Instead of using your rings, you can also buy cheap rings from local stores and use this for your project.

A silicone mold kit comes with easy instructions, but herewith a few easy steps:

There are two parts in the kit – parts A and B

Mix evenly (ratio 1:1) until the color looks even

The mixture can eventually be formed into a ball

Press down and flatten a little

Take your ring and press it into the mold

Leave for about 25 minutes and take it out

For the proper formation of the mold, there is a waiting period of about 48 hours, then you can add your resin

Common questions

Lifespan of resin rings

Resin rings should last for many years, depending on how well it was made and provided that you take good care of it. You can also check out our resin jewelry tutorial.

Tips to help your resin rings last longer

- Epoxy resins are one of the best products used in this process. Take into account if the resin is made for doming or molding and what is the best brand. The quality and type of resin that you use to make resin rings are very important to get the best results.
- It is natural for the resin to turn yellow over time. There are some products, which work better protecting your piece from yellowing.
- Resin rings must not be stored in direct sunlight, also avoid prolonged exposure to heat.
- Do not leave your ring in extreme heat such as direct sunlight in your car, as it can get damaged.
- All resin can scratch on the surface, so rather take it off if you are cleaning, doing dishes or do gardening.
- Creams, lotions, perfumes, and harsh chemicals (such as nail polish removers) often contain harmful chemicals. These cause permanent damage to your ring, so remove the ring before using these products.
- Store your resin ring in a cool, dark, airtight container.
- If you have made a mixed media ring, say with metal and resin, use high-quality metal as this will contribute to the lasting ability of your ring.

Epoxy Resin Lamp – Step by Step Resin Lamp Instructions

Making a resin lamp is a unique procedure that uses wood and epoxy resin. If you enjoy crafts and DIY, then making your own epoxy resin lamp can be a seriously rewarding process. This is a great combination of creating something useful for the house, as well as an artwork to admire. Let's unpack the process of how to make a resin lamp step by step, and uncover exactly what you will need to pay attention to when making an epoxy lamp.

The Idea Behind Resin Table Lamps

When it comes to making crafts, there are loads of different ways to get creative, upcycle old items, and make unique creations. The resin lamp became a popular idea on Pinterest, leading many people to attempt to make them. Making your own epoxy resin lamps is not that easy at first, and it will take some time to really master the art of it. Over time, you find your style and start to create quality, unique pieces. Looking on websites like Etsy can help massively with inspiration.

Equipment Needed for a Resin Wood Lamp

-
-
-
-
- Want to make your own resin table lamps? Here are some of the necessary
- supplies for creating these lamps.
-
- Epoxy resin
- Suitable wood
- Wood varnish
- Plexiglas
- An RGB LED light
- A module for this light
  Silicone glue
  Hot melting glue
  Sandpaper
  Polishing paste
  Hardener
  Wood wax
  Cable

How to Make a Resin Lamp – Step by Step Guide

Making a great resin lamp will require a few steps in order to achieve perfect results. Here are some processes to take when creating these items.

Getting the Wood Prepared

Before starting the work, preparation and planning are essential. First of all, you need to gather up some stumps of wood. You can order these online or buy them at a woodshop, but one of the best places is to gather up old oak stumps in the forest if this is a possibility. Just make sure that the wood stumps are of high quality, and won't rot or fall apart over time.

- Then it's time to cut down the wood pieces into the right shape and size for the lamp. Using a band saw to shape and cut the wood will really help. Once cut and prepared, it's a good idea to leave the wood to dry for a while. The longer you
- can let the wood dry out the better. There are a couple of different processes to follow when cleaning the wood. These are listed below:

- Simple clean:Use a scraper, knife, or metal brush to do a rough clean of the wood surface. Scrape off any mud, bark, lichen, and dirt of the wood. This can be a messy process so it's best done outside.
Deep clean:Once the wood is tidied up, you will need to really get deep in there with cleaning. Use an airstream compressor to make sure that the entire surface of the wood is completely clean.
Finishing:Once the wood is clean and dry, you can add a layer of varnish to enhance and protect the wood. Coat the pieces of wood with varnish, and leave them for at least 24 hours to dry completely.

Preparing the Lamp

While the wood is being left out to dry, you can start to prepare the work-piece for the lamp. Cut up some Plexiglas into pieces – the size of this should depend on the size of the lamp you are making. When figuring out how big to make the lamp, it' s always a good idea to design it according to the size of the room. If there is a lot of space that needs lighting up, then you will need to create a bigger lamp. Once the varnished wood is dry and ready, use a hot glue gun to stick the pieces of Plexiglas to the wooden base. The aim is to create a kind of box out of the Plexiglas with the piece of wood as the base.

Adding the Epoxy Resin

Now it' s time to start working with the epoxy resin. The first thing you need to do is weigh out the hardener and epoxy resin to the right proportions. Always check the manufacturer' s instructions here to make sure that you get the right mix ratio and consistency.

Once measured out, you can thoroughly mix the two components of the resin together. To make sure that you get the best mixture for your resin lamp, mix this for about 20 minutes, and strain it through a filter to get rid of any dust that may have collected.

Pour the resin into the lamp mold, and place this in the degasser. This is done to remove any bubbles that may form. Leave the item in the degasser for about an hour at 20 – 24 degrees Celcius. Once you take the resin out of the degasser, leave the item to cure fully at room temperature. The time this takes will vary depending on the resin and air temperature, but it should generally be left for around two days.

Finishing the Structure

When theresin has fully cured, the wood lamp is nearly ready. Once fully cured, you can remove the Plexiglas from the solid structure. This will leave you with the unfinished lamp. Cut some wood out the bottom and insert the LED light into here. This LED light should be the size of the lamp. You can use a manual milling machine to cut out this hole in the wood, and glue the LED light into the bottom. You will also need to make some holes under the lamp for adding the cable, and the soldered cable for the LED lamp. If you use an RGB LED light, you can control this with your phone via Bluetooth. This can be a really cool feature.

Then you need to join up the underside of the resin work-piece. This is best done with silicone glue and should be left for at least a full day to dry. Now the lamp is ready and dry, but the surface will be a bit uneven and rough. You can amend this by sanding down the entire surface. Start with 60 grit sandpaper, and slowly start to increase the size with each layer of sanding. Eventually, you can finish off the sanding with 2000 grit sandpaper. When hand sanding at the final stages, make the surface of the lamp slightly wet.

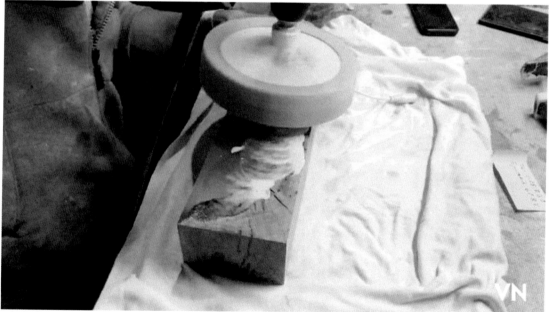

Finishing the Resin Lamp

Everything is all ready for use now. Before putting the lamp into place, there are just a few finishing touches that should be done.Polish the epoxy lamp's surface with some polishing paste that you can use on car headlights. Once polished, chafe the resin lamp with some wax. And there you have it, the lamp is complete and ready to use!

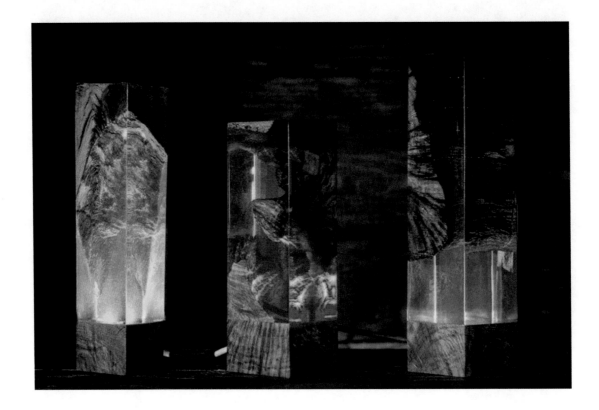

Making resin table lamps can be quite a time consuming and hands-on process. However, the results of your epoxy lamp masterpiece will be sure to have you feeling proud and happy with your work. Making a resin wood lamp is a satisfying process, and it will leave you with a product that you can enjoy for many years to follow.

How to make an Epoxy Resin River table with Wood [Tutorial]

© Comeback Images - stock.adobe.com

You think a beautiful epoxy table can only be obtained from a professional? Far from it! In the following tutorial we will show you in a step-by-step instruction and

with a detailed list of the required materials, how you can produce such a tasteful table yourself. And with the right materials and tools as well as practical tips, it's not as difficult as you might imagine.

What is behind the trend of epoxy resin river tables?

For some time now the trend around the artistic Epoxy River Tables has been on everyone's lips worldwide. The idea for these beautiful tables originated in the USA and started its triumphal procession all over the world from there. And not without reason: an epoxy river table is a small work of art that radiates luxury and modernity at the same time. So it fits into the living rooms of friends of rustic wooden furniture as well as in modern penthouse apartments.

Such a table simply cannot be put into any (style) drawer. The great popularity of Epoxy River Tables is probably also due to the fact that there are no limits to creativity. Rather traditionally designed tables with a neutral colour scheme can be found as well as exclusive, almost eccentric looking pieces in strong colours.

Ritesh Deora / shutterstock.com

Choosing the right wood

The key to making a truly beautiful Epoxy River Table is to choose the right wood to be used. Here it is undoubtedly worth digging a little deeper into your pocket in favour of a good quality material. After all, you want to put a lot of time and effort into your artwork and enjoy it for a long time.

The wood used should be as natural as possible. Here, for example, a board made from a tree trunk that is at least 4 cm thick is a good choice. A so-called "natural edge" with bark looks particularly stylish here. You can find such a piece of wood in a good carpenter's workshop, at a timber dealer or on the Internet.

Alternatively, you can of course use two wooden boards from the DIY store, which are cut into a slightly curved shape on one side with a jigsaw. Whether from a carpenter or from the DIY store: the most important thing is that the wood is well dried. Ideally the moisture content should be less than 12%.

Preparation of the wooden boards

You have two options for the preparation of the wood. Firstly, you can process the material itself. For this you need a circular saw and a planer to produce the right length and thickness and divide the wood in the middle.

On the other hand, you can of course also buy the boards in the desired thickness and length, or have your purchased piece of wood cut and planed to fit in a joinery. If you have little experience in processing wood, this is the much easier option. In addition, the possibly quite high purchase costs for the large machines are omitted. Even if your initial piece of wood is very large, it is advisable to have it prepared by a professional before you process it further.

Before proceeding further, you should make sure that your two boards are exactly the same length. In addition, the side edges must be cut at right angles to the straight outer sides. It is also important that both pieces of wood have the same thickness. They should also be absolutely flat. If in doubt, it is advisable to commission a joiner to carry out the finishing work.

Images: Vlad Teodor /Rawpixel.com / shutterstock.com

Creating the right working conditions

Since epoxy resin is a very sensitive material, ideal working conditions should be created before starting the processing.Very high temperatures, cold or humidity can have a negative effect on appearance and performance. In addition, unfavourable external conditions can affect the drying time of the resin.

The ideal temperature for processing epoxy resin is a constant minimum of 20° Celsius. This should also be considered during storage. Even if the room temperature is actually an ideal 20° C, the temperature drops significantly towards the floor. Here the thermometer can only show 15° to 17° C.

If the epoxy resin were to be stored on the floor at these temperatures, tiny, unsightly bubbles could quickly form in the resin. These cannot be removed so easily even with a hot air dryer. It is therefore better to store the material on a workbench or shelf. Another important factor is that the work area should also be dust-free, dry and well ventilated.

Create your own Epoxy River Table – step-by-step instructions

Step 1: Removing the bark and sanding the wood

- The first step is the thorough removal of any remaining bark, e.g. with a chisel. Although the bark looks very nice, it does not form an ideal bonding base for the epoxy resin. Then you should work the edges again by hand with sandpaper, so that wood and resin can later combine optimally.
- Now sand the large surfaces of the wood smoothly. An eccentric sander is particularly suitable for this. You should start with 80 grit and then work your way up to 220 grit. After each grit size the dust should be removed from the boards. The sides are best finished by hand with sandpaper.

- Finally, the wood must be cleaned extremely thoroughly from all dust residues. A vacuum cleaner is an excellent tool for this. Then wipe again with a microfibre cloth to get rid of the last fine sanding dust.

Images: left: Vlad Teodor / shutterstock.com, right:Velimir Isaevich/ shutterstock.com

Step 2: Fill in bumps and cracks and seal the wood

- Now all possible unevenness, cracks and porous areas in the wood must be levelled. These are simply filled with crystal clear, unpigmented epoxy resin. If you want to even out any unevenness in unfavourably located areas at the edges, you can seal the edges in advance with a very strong adhesive tape. This will prevent the resin from running over the edges afterwards.
- After the filled up resin has dried, the whole wood is sealed. Use a crystal-clear resin as you would for filling the cracks. This is generously distributed over the entire wood surface. This sealing prevents later outgassing of the wood.It is better to invest a little more money in a good brush that does not hair. Because once hairs have been distributed, it is very difficult to remove them from the resin again. The sealant must then dry very well. You should allow 5 hours for this in any case. The ideal temperature for drying is 18° to 24°C.
- After curing you should slightly roughen the inner edges, which will later come into contact with the cast resin, by hand with sandpaper. This will create the perfect base for the resin to bond with the edges.

Step 3: Build a mould / formwork for the table top

- Next, a mould is built in the desired length and size of the table. Simple MDF boards are used for this. The whole thing sounds more complicated than it actually is. However, it has to be measured and worked out very precisely and carefully. MDF boards with a thickness of 16 mm, both for the underside and the sides, have proven to be very suitable for the production of themould.
- The side panels should protrude the actual table top by approx. 15 mm. There are two possibilities for joining the underside with the side panels: either the individual parts can be screwed together or joined together with hot glue.

Images: left:brizmaker / shutterstock.com, right:Rawpixel.com / shutterstock.com

- To seal the edges afterwards, it is best to use clear sanitary silicone.Here, very careful work is essential to ensure that the mould is 100 % tight at the end. Otherwise liquid epoxy resin will leak out.
- Now areElease agentis applied in the finished mould.This is a very important step, as the resin could otherwise adhere to the MDF boards after drying. In this case it would be almost impossible to release the table top from the mould without damaging it. It would be possible to use adhesive tape to cover the entire mould or, alternatively, liquid release wax. Spraying with Teflon spray or silicone spray (this should be applied in up to three layers until the surface is smooth) is also suitable for this purpose.

Images: left:Wood - n Water Artwork and Design, right:Comeback Images/ shutterstock.com

Step 4: Inserting the wood into the mould

- Make sure that the work surface on which the mould rests is really 100% in the balance. Otherwise the resin would become skewed after filling and possibly leak. Once this has been ensured, the wood is now placed in the mould. To do this, the wood is pushed into the position that it should have when the table is finished and then fixed with several parallel clamps. If you are planning a slightly smaller model, the wood can alternatively be fixed with heavy objects such as stones. However, you should always bear in mind that any object used to fix the wood could come into contact with the resin.
- In order to prevent the resin from later being present on the entire table and not just in the gutter provided for it, it is advisable to draw a kind of barrier of sanitary silicone along the inner edges at a distance of 1 to 2 cm.

Step 5: Mix epoxy resin

Calculate the right amound of epoxy resin for your epoxy resin river table. This can be a little bit complicated. For this reason, we have created an epoxy resin calculator to help you out:

- In the next step you now mix the epoxy resin. Important: When working with resin please always wear safety glasses, breathing protection and nitrile gloves!
- Now you need a sufficiently large bucket. It would be ideal if this bucket holds the entire amount of resin or the first layer of resin. Please choose a sufficiently large bucket so that nothing can go wrong. It should also tend to be more wide than high, so that not too much heat is generated.
- This again shows that resin is a very sensitive material. From a certain amount and height it starts to get extremely hot and in extreme cases boils and thus becomes either cloudy or directly unusable. Therefore it may be necessary to cast the resin in several layers. The product used is the most important factor here. How many layers are required, or the maximum layer height and maximum amount to be mixed, ultimately depends on the thickness of your table top. If in doubt, observe the maximum layer thickness specified by the manufacturer or decide directly for a special epoxy resin as described above, which can be cast directly in one layer.

Images: left:Wood ‑ n Water Artwork and Design, right:futuristman/ shutterstock.com

- It is also particularly important that the mixing ratio recommended by the manufacturer is observedand that the individual components are then thoroughly mixed. A drill with a mixer attachment has proven to be the best solution for this.

-

After mixing , air bubbles that have formed in the resin can be easily removed with a Bunsen burner or hot air blow dryer . The rule here is: as much as necessary , as little as possible. If the resin is heated too much, it will be damaged.

Step 6: Colouring the resin Creating a water effect

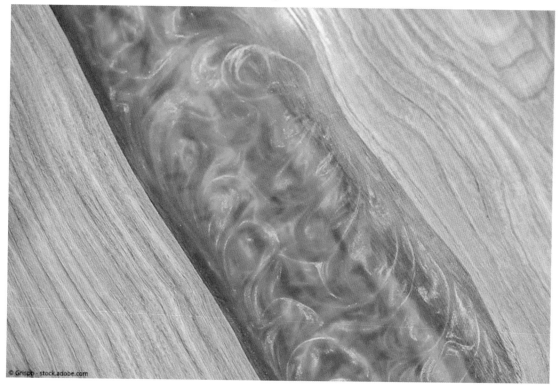

- Especially when casting a water effect, it becomes clear why the acquisition of a special epoxy resin, which can be cast very easily in one step, pays off.

- If you want to achieve the popular water look after mixing the two resin components, the appropriate colour pigments must now be added to the epoxy resin. To do this, divide the resin into two containers (the ratio 1:1.5 would be possible, for example). To achieve the water effect, colour the larger part of the resin with a metallic pigment in turquoise and the smaller part with a matt blue pigment. This mixture refers, as said, only to the typical water look. In general, there are no limits to the choice of colour.

- When filling in the epoxy resin there are again two possibilities. You can either pour the resin from the two containers alternately into the mould or simultaneously from one side each. Slight circular movements, especially with the metallic epoxy resin, make the final result look lively.

- At the end, the resulting pattern can be changed with a wooden stick or similar.

Afterwards the epoxy resin has to cure very well (follow the manufacturer's instructions).

Images: left:© Suteren Studio – stock.adobe.com, right:Suteren/ shutterstock.com

Step 7: Creating a design with crystal clear resin

- In addition to the typical water look, there is an infinite number of different designs that turn your DIY table into a real work of art.Just as nice to look at is for example a River Table with crystal clear resin and embedded objects. For this, a first layer of crystal clear resin is poured between the two wooden boards. This process should be done very quickly, but still carefully.

- Afterwards a short (!) walk over the epoxy resin with a hot air dryer.Extreme caution is required here. If the resin is exposed to the extreme heat of the hairdryer at the same spot for longer than 3 seconds, this can cause, among other things, a burning of the material. The final result is an unsightly yellow epoxy.

Images: left:Marco Zamperini / shutterstock.com,right:Wood ᵔ n Water Artwork and Design

*

Now follows the so-called "B Stage", the second layer.When this layer is poured, the first layer should not yet be completely dry and still slightly sticky on the surface. You must not miss this point, as the next layer can only bond optimally with the first one if the substrate is slightly sticky. If the first layer is already
• completely dry, wait until the resin is completely cured. Then sand the surface with a 220 grain, clean it thoroughly and then pour the second layer.

If you want to embed decorative elements such as crystals or pebbles in the epoxy
• resin, then these should be added to the second layer. This has the advantage that they can no longer sink to the bottom.

Now the resin layer can be filled in to just above the edge and then allowed to dry completely again. The manufacturer's instructions should again be observed.

Step 8: Removal from the mould and sanding

Next, the cast table top is released from the mould. To do this, remove all screws and parallel clamps and carefully loosen the table top from the mould using a chisel and a plastic hammer.Afterwards the table top can be ground. This work can be done by hand. However, an orbital sander makes the task incredibly easier. Start with an 80 grit and work your way up to 400 grit. At the end there should be no more resin on the wood.

For perfectly smooth edges, these can be additionally processed with a router before sanding or, if necessary, cleanly re-cut or planed again with a circular saw. However, these steps are not absolutely necessary. A small tip: The higher the grain of the sanding paper, the lighter the surface of the Epoxy River Table will be at the end.

Images:Comeback Images/ shutterstock.com

Step 9: Finishing / finishing

Polishing and oiling the table top

Now follows the finish, in order to protect the wood optimally. On the one hand you have the possibility to achieve a natural, matt look. To achieve this, the finished table top – and especially the resin river – should be thoroughly polished with a polishing machine and polishing paste. This procedure ensures that all traces of sanding are removed and a silky surface is achieved.

For a matt appearance, oil is then applied evenly over the entire table top, e.g. with a soft cloth. This method is extremely simple and seals the wood perfectly. In addition, only one single application is required here.

For the epoxy resin polishing we have prepared separate, detailed instructions.

Images: left:Osadchaya Olga/ shutterstock.com,right:© Suteren Studio – stock.adobe.com

-
Covering with crystal clear resin

If you prefer a glossy look, you can instead coat the surface of the table top with crystal-clear resin. To do this, start with the underside of the table top and first apply a sturdy adhesive tape around the top, which should protrude 1 to 2 cm. This prevents the resin from dripping down the sides.

Now the resin is poured over the surface and evenly distributed over the entire surface. A plastic spatula, for example, is suitable for this. Go briefly over the resin with a hot air dryer to avoid bubbles. Afterwards, the whole thing must be completely hardened again.

-

Since the first layer is only the base, you should always pour a second layer of resin. Here too , the first layer should be sanded briefly to ensure a successful bond between the two layers.

-
After curing, you can now remove the adhesive tape on the sides. Now the edge of the painted underside is taped (at least 5 cm wide).

-
Then you can turn the table top over and put something suitable underneath it, such as leftover pieces of wood. To avoid damage to the lacquered side, you should also place a fleece underneath.

The table top must be 100% level again, so that the resin can now be poured over the top of the table. After the subsequent distribution with a spatula and the drying time, the remaining adhesive tape can now be removed and all sharp edges can be sanded with a fine sandpaper.

Images: Wood ⁻ n Water Artwork and Design / www.woodnwater.com.br

-

Spraying by professionals with polyurethane lacquer

For a perfect, mirror-smooth surface, a professional must be commissioned after all, because a polyurethane coating is necessary for this. Such a paint job can only be done with special equipment, a paint booth and a lot of know-how. Furthermore, this technique is very cost-intensive. The advantage of a polyurethane paint would be a very high durability and insensitivity, e.g. to scratch marks. However, with such a high-quality piece as the self-built Epoxy River Table, the investment in such a painting is worth considering in any case.

Last but not least: Attach the table legs

- In order to finally finish the good piece you can screw on legs of your choice. With classic wooden legs, the table looks rustic, but at the same time noble. Stylish metal table legs turn the table into a modern piece of furniture.

How to Make Silicone Molds: A Practical Guide

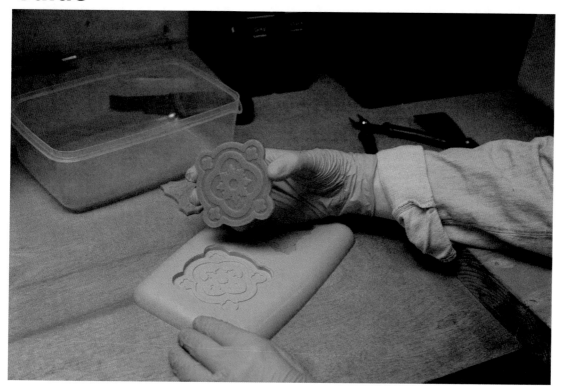

Throughout history, artisans have used molds to make everything from Bronze Age weaponry to modern-day consumer products. While early molds were commonly shaped in stone, modern science has given rise to materials that are far easier to work with, such as silicone.

Today, a vast array of industries rely on silicone molding. Product developers, engineers, DIY makers, and even chefs all make silicone molds to create one-off or smaller runs of parts.

In this practical guide to silicone mold-making, we'll break down everything you need to know before getting started, provide a list of items you'll need, and give you a step-by-step guide for incorporating silicone molds into any type of project.

Why Make Silicone Molds?

Silicone is a strong choice for mold-making because it offers such a diverse array of benefits. You can easily create custom designs using silicone molding. The molds themselves are also quite durable, so you can use them repeatedly without fear of breakage. Silicone's inorganic makeup—compared to rubber, its organic counterpart—makes it highly resilient to heat and cold, chemical exposure, and even fungus. Some of the benefits of silicone molds include the following:

Flexibility

Silicone's flexibility makes it easy to work with. Silicone molds are pliable and lightweight compared to stiffer substances like plastic and they're also easier to remove once a part is fully formed. Thanks to silicone's high level of flexibility, both the mold and the fabricated part are less likely to break or chip. You can use custom silicone molds to shape everything from complex engineering components to holiday-themed ice cubes or confections.

Stability

Silicone withstands <u>temperatures</u> from -65° to 400° degrees Celsius. Additionally, it can have an elongation of 700%, depending on the formulation. Highly stable under a broad range of conditions, you can put silicone molds in the oven, freeze them, and stretch them during removal.

Durability

In most cases, you'll get many runs out of a silicone mold. However, it's important to note that the life span of molds can vary greatly. The more frequently you cast, and the more complex or detailed your design, the faster your mold might degrade. To maximize the life of your silicone molds, clean them with mild soap and water, dry them thoroughly, and store them flat without stacking.

Limitations

While there are a lot of benefits to working with silicone, there are also a few limitations to be aware of:

- Silicone costs more than latex and organic rubbers. A quick comparison on Amazon shows a gallon of silicone regularly topping $100—almost twice as much as latex.

- Though it's flexible, silicone can tear if stretched too far.

- Not all silicone is formulated equally. Always purchase silicone and any manufacturing materials from a reputable supplier.

How To Make Patterns for Silicone Molding

A pattern—sometimes referred to as a master—is the part you use to create a precise negative in your silicone mold. If you are simply trying to replicate an existing object, it might make sense to use that object as your pattern. You'll just need to be sure that the object can withstand the mold-making process.

To create a new design or prototype, you must first fabricate your pattern; you have several options for this. Here are a few ways to make patterns for silicone molding:

- Sculpting – If you're a talented sculptor or if you're creating a relatively simple design, you can use clay to create a pattern. Sculpting a pattern is also a fun project for kids and a cost-effective option for DIYers.

- Carving – You can make your pattern out of wood. Carved wood masters are an excellent choice for making tiles and flat designs.

- <u>3D printing</u>– Many professionals and commercial designers choose to 3D print patterns. <u>Desktop 3D printers</u> offer many benefits, including design flexibility within CAD software, high accuracy, ease of prototype modification, and quick turnaround times.

Once you have a pattern, you can get started with making your silicone mold.

Getting Started with Silicone Mold-Making

Here's everything you'll need to build a basic silicone molding kit:

- A master pattern

- Liquid silicone, such as Smooth-On OOMOO 30

- A box or nonporous container for the mold housing Mold

- release, such as Smooth-On universal mold release Wax, resin, or

- other end-use material

One-Piece vs. Two-Piece Silicone Molds

Before you start making your molds, you' ll need to determine which type of mold(s) you want to create.

One-piece silicone molds are like ice cube trays. You fill the mold and then let the material set . However, just as an ice cube tray creates cubes with a flat top, one-piece molds will only work with designs that have a flat side. If your master has deep undercuts, that also makes it harder to remove it and the finished parts from the mold once the silicone sets without damage.

When these are not a concern for your design, a one-piece silicone mold is an ideal way to create a seamless 3D reproduction of your master on all of its other surfaces.

One-piece silicone molds are ideal for designs that have a flat side and no deep undercuts.

A two-piece silicone mold is better for reproducing your 3D master without a flat side or has deep undercuts. The mold splits into two pieces that join back together, forming a fillable 3D cavity (similar to how injection molding works).

Two-piece molds leave no flat surfaces and are easier to work with than single block molds. On the downside, they are a bit more complex to create and seams may form if the two pieces aren' t perfectly flush.

Two-piece silicone molds can reproduce any master design. (image source)

How to Make Silicone Molds

First, you' ll need to decide if you want to use a one-piece or two-piece mold. The processes for making these molds are similar, but it will take a bit longer to create a two-part mold. You can use the following step-by-step instruction to create your own silicone molds.

One-Piece Silicone Mold

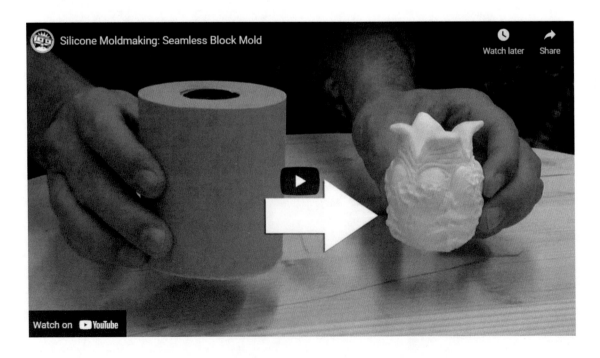

Silicone Moldmaking: Seamless Block Mold

Watch later   Share

Watch on ▶ YouTube

1. Create your product master: This is your final part design, which will be replicated in another material. When 3D printing on a stereolithography (SLA) 3D printer, use any Standard Resin with a layer height of 50 microns. Keep the detailed surface free of support marks. Wash the parts thoroughly with IPA—any residual tackiness on the surface can affect the silicone molding process.

2. Construct the mold housing: Coated MDF is a popular choice for constructing a containment box for the silicone mold, but even a simple premade plastic container will do. Look for nonporous materials and a flat bottom.

3. Lay out the master and apply mold release: Start by lightly misting the inside of the mold housing with mold release. Tile the masters inside the box with the detailed side up. Lightly spray these with mold release as well. This will need about 10 minutes to dry thoroughly.

4. Prepare the silicone: Mix the silicone rubber according to the package instructions. You can use a vibrating device like a handheld electric sander to remove air bubbles.

5. Pour the silicone into the mold housing : Gently pour the mixed silicone rubber into the containment box in a narrow stream . Aim for the lowest part of the box first (the base) and gradually come up the contours of your 3D printed master. Cover it with at least one centimeter of silicone . The curing process will take from one hour to one day to complete , depending on the silicone type and brand.

6. De-mold the silicone: When curing is complete, peel the silicone out of the containment box and remove the masters. This will serve as your ice cube tray- style mold for casting your end-use product.

7. Cast your part: Again, it' s a good idea to lightly spray the silicone mold with mold release and let it dry for 10 minutes . Pour your end -use material (wax or concrete , for example) into the cavities , and allow to cure.

8. Prepare the mold for the next casting: You can use this silicone mold multiple times. Return to step seven to repeat the process.

Two-Piece Silicone Mold

To create a two-part mold, start by following the first two steps above, which include creating a master and constructing the mold housing. After that, follow this process to create a two-part mold:

1. Lay out the masters in clay: Use the clay to form what will eventually be one half of your mold. The clay should be placed inside your mold housing with half of your master sticking out of the clay.

2. Prepare and pour your silicone: Follow the package instructions included with your silicone to prepare and gently pour the silicone into your mold housing on top of the clay and your masters. This layer of silicone will be one half of your two-piece mold.

3. Remove everything from the mold housing: Once your first mold has cured, you'll need to remove the silicone mold, masters, and clay from the mold housing. It's okay if the layers separate upon extraction.

4. Clean away the clay: Clean all of the clay away to reveal your first silicone mold and masters. Make sure your masters and your existing mold are completely clean.

5. Place the mold and masters back in the mold housing: Insert both your existing silicone mold and the masters (laid in the mold) back into the mold housing facing up instead of down.

6. Apply release agent: Apply a thin layer of release agent to the top of your master and existing silicone mold to make de-molding easier.

7. Prepare and pour the silicone for your second mold: Following the same instructions as before, prepare and pour the silicone into the mold housing to create your second mold.

8. Wait for your second mold to cure: Allow plenty of time for your second mold to cure before attempting to remove it from the mold housing.

9. De-mold your parts: Remove both silicone molds from the mold housing and gently pull them apart.